The South Carolina Colony

KEVIN CUNNINGHAM

Children's Press®
An Imprint of Scholastic Inc.
New York Toronto London Auckland Sydney
Mexico City New Delhi Hong Kong
Danbury, Connecticut

Content Consultant
Jeffrey Kaja, PhD
Associate Professor of History
California State University, Northridge

Library of Congress Cataloging-in-Publication Data

Cunningham, Kevin, 1966–
  The South Carolina colony/Kevin Cunningham.
      p. cm.—(A true book)
  Includes bibliographical references and index.
  ISBN-13: 978-0-531-25398-4 (lib. bdg.)   ISBN-13: 978-0-531-26611-3 (pbk.)
  ISBN-10: 0-531-25398-4 (lib. bdg.)   ISBN-10: 0-531-26611-3 (pbk.)
  1. South Carolina—Juvenile literature. I. Title. II. Series.
  F269.3.C86 2011
  975.7—dc22   2011010881

All rights reserved. Published in 2012 by Children's Press, an imprint of Scholastic Inc.
Printed in China 62
SCHOLASTIC, CHILDREN'S PRESS, A TRUE BOOK, and associated logos are trademarks and/or registered trademarks of Scholastic Inc.
1 2 3 4 5 6 7 8 9 10 R 21 20 19 18 17 16 15 14 13 12

Find the Truth!

Everything you are about to read is true *except* for one of the sentences on this page.

Which one is **TRUE**?

T or F People from western and eastern South Carolina often disagreed.

T or F The French were the first Europeans to settle in South Carolina.

Find the answers in this book.

Contents

**Hernando de Soto and a
Native American leader**

THE BIG TRUTH!

South Carolina's Founding Fathers

List of South Carolina royal land grants

What experiences did these three founders share? **38**

Pirates once held hostage a ship full of Charles Town residents.

5

Timeline of South Carolina Colony History

10,000 B.C.E.

Early Native Americans settle in present-day South Carolina and the surrounding regions.

1521

Spanish explorer Francisco Gordillo lands in South Carolina.

1680

Charles Town is founded.

1759

South Carolina settlers battle the Cherokee.

1788

South Carolina approves the U.S. Constitution.

CHAPTER 1

The Native Americans

About 30 groups of native peoples inhabited South Carolina long before Europeans came to the region. The Catawba worked as farmers. Carolina Souian groups such as the Chicora built villages near the coast of the Atlantic Ocean and in the region's north and east. The Cherokee lived in dozens of villages along the Appalachian Mountains to the west. Members of the Yamasee tribe moved into the area centuries later. They had been driven out of neighboring Georgia by European settlers.

The Cherokee

Native groups in the Carolina region depended on farming as a major source of food.

A Cherokee family usually included grandparents, parents, and children. A typical Cherokee village had between 30 and 60 houses. They were built around a council house used for meetings and religious ceremonies. Women were responsible for planting and tending fields of maize (corn), squash, and beans. They also turned deerskin into leather by soaking it in water. The softened skin was then stretched and dried before being made into clothing.

The Cherokee made dugout canoes by hollowing out a tree trunk.

Men hunted deer and other game with wooden bows and arrows. Cherokee used the meat and skins of animals. They also crafted animal bones and antlers into tools, needles, and combs. They fished with wooden traps and nets. Other native peoples along the coast gathered seafood such as oysters. They used canoes to fish away from the shore. Women often gathered berries, nuts, and other wild plants.

Appalachian Mountains

Original
13 Colonies

Area
enlarged

Cowpens
King's
Mountain

NORTH CAROLINA

CHEROKEE

Fort Prince George

CATAWBA

Cheraw

Pee Dee River

Saluda River

Broad Run

Camden

Pee Dee

Ninety Six

Columbia

SOUTH CAROLINA

Fort Motte

GEORGIA

Savannah River

Orangeburg

Congaree River

Georgetown

Edisto R.

Fort Edisto

WANDO

EDISTO

STONO

Charles Town

Fort Sullivan

Beaufort

Port Royal

Hilton Head Island

Savannah

ATLANTIC OCEAN

miles   50

km   50

Colonial boundaries

Present boundaries

CHAPTER 2

Explorers and Colonists

The Spanish started colonies in the Caribbean in 1493. The colonists immediately turned the native peoples into slaves. Many Indians died from the diseases the Europeans had brought with them. The Spanish soon sailed to North America in search of new slaves. Francisco Gordillo went ashore in June 1521. He named the land Carolana, which means "land of Charles," after Spain's king.

Chicora warriors lead an attack against Ayllón and his men.

Gordillo kidnapped several Chicora people and sent them to the Caribbean. One of the Chicora learned Spanish. He told a judge named Lucas Vázquez de Ayllón that the Chicora's land was full of gold. Ayllón went back to Carolana with Chicora slaves in 1526 to search for the treasure. The Indians were now back in their homeland. They quickly ran away. Ayllón built the first European town in the region to continue his search. But sickness killed him and many of his men.

Death and Disease

Spanish explorer Hernando de Soto traveled through Cherokee lands around 1540 in search of gold. His men killed and enslaved some Cherokee. Deadly diseases brought by the Spaniards may have killed three out of four Cherokee people in the region.

The local peoples often attacked European settlers after this. Spain and France stopped attempting to settle the area by the 1580s. But England would succeed eighty years later where the Spanish and French had failed.

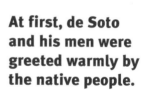

At first, de Soto and his men were greeted warmly by the native people.

Smallpox

European diseases such as smallpox and measles killed many more Native Americans than guns did. Historians believe that smallpox may have been the deadliest of all the diseases. The virus causes fever, bleeding, and a rash of painful red sores that cover the body. Many European explorers had been exposed to smallpox as children. They could resist the disease. But Native Americans had never encountered it. Their bodies were unable to protect them from the virus.

This list of land grants was written in 1674.

The English Arrive

King Charles II of England appointed eight men **proprietors** of a new **colony** in North America in 1663. He called it Carolina. Its goal was to make money for England and the proprietors by selling and renting land to settlers. The proprietors offered land cheaply to attract settlers. They also wrote a series of laws called the Fundamental Constitutions. These laws gave landowners the right to elect representatives to a **legislature**.

Parts of Charles Town's early settlements have been rebuilt.

The proprietors hoped to bring in settlers by claiming to offer religious freedom. This promise set Carolina apart from most of Europe. Religious **prejudice** was common there. The proprietors sent 100 settlers to a site near Port Royal by 1670. The settler ships moved up the coast to the Kiawah River after a warning from friendly local Indians. They built cabins and a dock for a settlement they called Charles Town, known today as Charleston. They settled in this safer place in 1680.

Disasters Strike

About 1,000 English settlers had cut down forests to create farms and build settlements by then. But relations with some Native Americans grew tense as the English continued to claim native land. Settlers often cheated Native Americans when trading with them. They also made money selling Indians into slavery. Charles Town also experienced several disasters. Fire destroyed half its houses in 1698. A hurricane also badly damaged the town.

The Yamasee fought a war against settlers from 1715 until 1716.

Charles Town quickly became a thriving port with goods being shipped to England.

Making Money

The port of Charles Town helped the settlement recover. Trading ships sailed to England with meat and wood products such as barrels. New **cash crops** boosted Carolina's profits after 1700. The most important was rice. Rice grew well in the hot, wet weather. Growing rice required a lot of work. Owners of large farms called plantations began to bring in slaves to work the land.

Slaves in the Colony

Settlers had used enslaved Native Americans as labor in the past. Colonists soon came to rely on enslaved people from Africa and the West Indies. Charles Town became a major city for buying and selling enslaved Africans. Slaves soon outnumbered Europeans in the colony. Most enslaved people worked on plantations. Smaller farmers sometimes owned a few slaves too. Slaves also sometimes worked as assistants to skilled tradesmen such as carpenters.

Rice was grown successfully in South Carolina as early as 1680.

Slaves harvest rice on a Carolina rice field.

Enemies Everywhere

Charles Town's success made it a frequent target of enemies. Spanish and French ships attacked the settlement in 1706. The colony called out its **militia** and turned back the invaders. Clashes over land and the enslavement of Indians erupted into a two-year war between the colonists and the Yamasee in 1715. A fleet of pirate ships commanded by Edward Teach, or Blackbeard, began to attack ships entering and leaving the city shortly after the war.

Blackbeard's career as a pirate captain lasted only two years.

South Carolina's Fort Johnson was built in 1704 to protect the Charles Town harbor and settlement.

Becoming a Royal Colony

Carolina's militia and the Cherokee drove the Yamasee into Florida. The British navy put an end to Teach. But the colonists complained that the proprietors had done little to help them. The colony had already split into northern and southern Carolina by that time. Southern settlers asked the British king to take control of the colony and protect it. North and South Carolina became separate royal colonies under the protection of Great Britain in 1729.

CHAPTER 3

Living and Working

South Carolina's economy relied on farming and trade. The wealthy plantation owners and merchants at the top of society copied British fashions and ways. They enjoyed afternoon teas and sent their sons to English universities. The wealthy built huge plantation mansions in Charles Town. These mansions were filled with art and expensive furniture. Wealthy colonists threw parties in the summer that featured music and feasts prepared by servants and enslaved workers.

The South Carolina upper class included some of the richest people in the colonies.

Approximately 1,800 German settlers arrived in South Carolina in 1752.

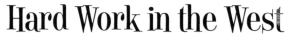

Hard Work in the West

The British government invited new farmers to settle the rural lands west of Charles Town as the 1700s continued. Settlers from Germany, the Netherlands, and Ireland took an offer of 50 acres (20 hectares) of land in return for clearing the forest for farms. These farmers worked many hours a day. They lived in cabins or in cottages with dirt floors. Few roads existed to connect farmers to towns or other families.

Women on the Farm

Farm women cared for the children and the house. They cooked and prepared food for winter storage. They also spun flax and cotton into yarn. Many of them made clothes and kept vegetable gardens. Mothers also cared for the sick. Some women found time to make products such as herbal medicines to sell for extra money.

Some frontier families were fortunate enough to own a loom to make their own cloth.

Men's Work

Few rural farmers owned slaves. The men plowed and planted. They raised livestock and harvested the crops. The men and their sons brought grains such as wheat and maize to nearby mills. The grain was ground into flour for use at home or to sell. Men and boys also hunted deer and other animals in the woods. Meat from their livestock and deer fed the family. Animal skins were made into clothing.

Building a cabin near a waterway gave a settler access to transportation.

 Enslaved family members were often sold to different owners.

Slave Life

South Carolina's thousands of enslaved people lived without any rights or freedoms. Owners worked them and sold them as they pleased. The children of slaves were also considered slaves. Slaves could be beaten for failing to work as hard as the owners wanted or simply for speaking without permission.

Owners often hired out their enslaved workers to others. They kept most or all of the slaves' earnings for themselves.

A crowd disrupts an election in Charles Town.

28

CHAPTER 4

Fighting for Freedom

South Carolina colonists came into conflict with each other as the 1700s continued. The colony leaders were the plantation owners and merchants in Charles Town. Charles Town was located in the east on the Atlantic Coast. Western farmers believed these leaders ignored their problems and passed unfair taxes. Western settlers insisted on more representatives in the colony's legislature. They also demanded that the colony help them deal with attacks by the Cherokee.

New Taxes, New Anger

From 1754 to 1763, Britain and its Native American **allies** fought France and its native allies for control of North America. This conflict became known as the French and Indian War. The British won the war. But they had gone into debt to pay for the war and to build forts to protect the colonies. Parliament, the British legislature, needed to raise money. It placed a tax on many items important to the colonies' economies. Many Carolinians already had difficulties making enough money.

Colonial militias fought alongside the British during the French and Indian War. →

A Carolina colonist forces a tax collector off her property.

A tax on sugar in 1764 was unpopular with the colonists. But the Stamp Act of 1765 created harsh feelings toward England. The tax forced American colonists to buy a stamp for all printed material, including newspapers and legal documents. Crowds gathered throughout the colonies to protest. In Charles Town, British troops hid the stamps in a fort to prevent colonists from destroying them. Antitax forces protested with a **boycott** of British goods.

Colonists accepted taxes paid to the colony because they elected representatives who passed the tax laws. But Americans had no representatives in Parliament to defend their interests against British taxes. Colonial newspapers and antitax speakers called this "taxation without representation." Parliament canceled the Stamp Act in early 1766. But more taxes came and went in the late 1760s. A tax on tea remained.

Benjamin Franklin visited Parliament to talk its member into ending the Stamp Act.

Colonists dump British tea off ships during the Boston Tea Party.

A British company was allowed to sell its tea without paying a tax. But American tea companies continued to pay it. A group called the Sons of Liberty protested in 1773 by dumping British tea into Boston Harbor. The event became known as the Boston Tea Party. The next year, representatives from 12 colonies met at the First Continental Congress in Philadelphia to decide what to do about the colonies' strained relationship with Britain.

Francis Marion, nicknamed the Swamp Fox, commanded some of South Carolina's troops.

Francis Marion and his soldiers cross the Pee Dee River in South Carolina, on their way to attack British troops.

The American Revolutionary War began on April 19, 1775. Massachusetts militiamen fought British soldiers outside Boston. South Carolina's **Patriot** government immediately organized soldiers to defend the colony. They soon took control of Charles Town's harbor to block the British navy. Many rural farmers were pro-British **Loyalists**. They distrusted their fellow colonists in Charles Town more than they did Britain.

The Gadsden Flag

Loyalists and Patriots fought each other in the west as British officials fled Charles Town. Patriots from across the colony voted on a **constitution**. It created a new South Carolina government. Patriot leader Christopher Gadsden rushed home from the Second Continental Congress in May 1775 when he heard rumors of a British attack on Charles Town. He brought a flag that he designed. On it was a picture of a rattlesnake with the warning Dont Tread on Me.

The rattlesnake was a popular American symbol during the time of the Revolutionary War.

Christopher Gadsden

Christopher Gadsden was a successful merchant and fought in the Cherokee War of 1759–1761. He later led a Sons of Liberty group in Charles Town. Gadsden stayed in the town when the British captured it in 1780. The British sent him to Florida as a prisoner of war. He was released 10 months later. The prison term weakened him so much that he turned down the chance to be South Carolina's governor in 1782.

South Carolina's state flag is based on a flag used at Sullivan's Island.

On June 28, 1776, Gadsden's flag flew alongside other colonial flags at the Battle of Sullivan's Island outside Charles Town. South Carolina's cannons forced the British out. The war was mostly fought in the north for the next three years. The British returned to Charles Town in March 1780 with more than 13,000 men and 90 ships. Five thousand Patriots held out for six weeks before surrendering. British troops were aided by Loyalists. They marched further into South Carolina.

South Carolina's Founding Fathers

The earliest battles of the American Revolutionary War had already taken place when the Second Continental Congress met on May 10, 1775. Many representatives hoped at first that the colonies could reach a peaceful understanding with Britain. By June 1776, the Congress had assigned a five-man committee to write a document stating the colonies' intention to break away from England. The Declaration of Independence was approved by 12 of the 13 colonies on July 4, 1776. New York added its vote on July 15th. Four South Carolina representatives signed the declaration. Here are three.

Thomas Heyward

Thomas Heyward was a lawyer and farmer. He took part in Patriot actions before the war. The British captured him at Charles Town in 1780. He served in South Carolina's state government and as a judge after the war.

Arthur Middleton

Arthur Middleton was a plantation owner educated in Britain. He replaced his famous father, Henry, at the Second Continental Congress. Like Thomas Heyward and Edward Rutledge, he spent the late part of the war in a British prison.

Edward Rutledge

Edward Rutledge was 26 years old when he became the youngest person to sign the Declaration of Independence. He was captured at Charles Town and shared the same prison as Arthur Middleton. He later served in the state government and spent a year as South Carolina's governor.

A new general named Nathanael Greene took charge in the south. What followed turned the war in the Americans' favor. On January 17, 1781, American Continental army troops destroyed part of the British forces at Cowpens, South Carolina. The rest of the British chased Greene across North Carolina. In October, a combination of George Washington's Continentals and his French allies trapped the British in Yorktown, Virginia. The surrender of the British at Yorktown convinced Parliament to end the war.

The Battle of Cowpens was an important victory for American troops.

The British left Charles Town in December 1782, four months after the Battle of Yorktown.

The Americans had won. But South Carolina's economy lay in ruins. Many South Carolinians had died in the war. Failed businesses left many people out of work. Loyalists and Patriots had destroyed each other's farms. Thousands of slaves had left the colonies with the British. This left few workers on the plantations. There was also still bitterness between settlers in the rural areas and those in Charles Town.

The new nation had to decide whether it wanted a strong national government. Representatives of 12 states met in Philadelphia in 1787 to write a constitution that would create a government and also limit its powers. The new U.S. Constitution was then sent to each state for approval. South Carolina accepted the document on May 23, 1788. It became the eighth state of the United States of America. ★

 All four South Carolinians to sign the Constitution were wealthy landowners.

Number of proprietors who owned Carolina: 8

Fraction of Charles Town destroyed by fire in 1698: One-half

Year South Carolina became a royal colony: 1729

Number of acres offered to new backcountry settlers: 50

Slave population in South Carolina in 1750: Almost 40,000

Number of colonies that sent representatives to the First Continental Congress: 12

Number of South Carolinians who signed the Declaration of Independence: 4

Number of British forces at the 1780 attack on Charles Town: More than 13,000

Number of American forces at the 1780 attack on Charles Town: 5,000

Did you find the truth?

T People from western and eastern South Carolina often disagreed.

F The French were the first Europeans to settle in South Carolina.

Resources

Books

Blashfield, Jean F. *The South Carolina Colony*. North Mankato, MN: Child's World, 2004.

Glaser, Jason. *South Carolina*. New York: PowerKids, 2010.

Haberle, Susan E. *The South Carolina Colony*. Mankato, MN: Capstone, 2006.

Hazen, Walter A. *Everyday Life: Colonial Times*. Culver City, CA: Good Year Books, 2008.

Kaufman, Scott. *Francis Marion: Swamp Fox of South Carolina*. Stockton, NJ: OTTN, 2007.

Marsh, Carole. *South Carolina Native Americans*. Peachtree City, GA: Gallopade International, 2004.

Santella, Andrew. *The Cherokee*. New York: Children's Press, 2001.

Weatherly, Myra S. *South Carolina*. New York: Children's Press, 2009.

Organizations and Web Sites

Cherokee Nation

www.cherokee.org

Learn about Cherokee history and culture, and find out what's going on today on the Cherokee Reservation in Tahlequah, Oklahoma.

South Carolina Historical Society

www.southcarolinahistoricalsociety.org

Get more information on South Carolina history by searching an online collection of photographs and documents.

Places to Visit

Charleston Museum

360 Meeting Street
Charleston, SC 29403
(843) 722-2996
www.charlestonmuseum.org
Study exhibits on South Carolina's native peoples, colonists, and Revolutionary War battles at the oldest museum in the United States.

Old Exchange and Provost Dungeon

122 East Bay Street
Charleston, SC 29401
(843) 727-2165
www.oldexchange.com
This historic building, built in 1771, was used by Patriots to create South Carolina's government and by the British as a jail.

Important Words

allies (AL-eyes) — people or countries that are on the same side during a war or disagreement

boycott (BOI-kaht) — a refusal to buy goods from a person, group, or country

cash crops (KASH KROPS) — crops grown for sale rather than for a family's own use

colony (KAH-luh-nee) — an area settled by people from another country and controlled by that country

constitution (kahn-sti-TOO-shun) — the laws of a country that state the rights of the people and the powers of government

legislature (LEJ-is-lay-chur) — a body with the power to make or change laws

Loyalists (LOI-uhl-ists) — American colonists who remained faithful to Great Britain's rule

militia (muh-LISH-uh) — a group of people who are trained to fight but who aren't professional soldiers

Patriot (PAY-tree-uht) — an American colonist opposed to Great Britain

prejudice (PREJ-uh-dis) — unreasonable or unfair opinion based on a person's religion, race, or other characteristic

proprietors (pro-PRI-eh-torz) — people granted ownership of a colony

Index

Page numbers in **bold** indicate illustrations

About the Author

Kevin Cunningham has written more than 40 books on disasters, the history of disease, Native Americans, and other topics. Cunningham lives near Chicago with his wife and young daughter.